An Insider's Guide to Accident & Injury Law in Missouri & Kansas

AF882753

CRASH COURSE: 9 MISTAKES THAT CAN WRECK YOUR INJURY CLAIM

K|J|M

LAW OFFICE OF
KEVIN J. MCMANUS

Kevin J. McManus
Law Office of Kevin J. McManus
1100 Main Street, Suite 2620
Kansas City, MO 64105
www.KevinMcManusLaw.com
816-203-0143

Copyright © 2018 by Kevin J. McManus
1st Edition

All Rights Reserved. This report may not be used or reproduced in any manner without the written permission and consent of the author.

Printed in the United States of America.

ISBN: 978-0-692-16001-5
$16.95

If you can answer YES to these questions, our firm may be able to help you.

1. Do you have total expected medical bills and lost wages (not just out-of-pocket expenses) of at least $3,000?

2. Was the accident the fault of someone else?

3. Was there visible damage to your car?

4. Did you seek medical treatment soon after the accident?

5. Are you following the recommended treatment of your doctor?

6. Did the accident occur less than two years ago?

If you answered YES to each of these questions, please call us at 816-203-0143.

K|J|M

LAW OFFICE OF
KEVIN J. MCMANUS

1100 Main Street, Suite 2620
Kansas City, MO 64105
www.KevinMcManusLaw.com
816-203-0143

LEGAL DISCLAIMERS:
THE INFORMATION IN THIS REPORT CONTAINS GENERAL STATEMENTS AND IS NOT INTENDED AS LEGAL ADVICE OR LEGAL OPINIONS. THIS REPORT DOES NOT CREATE AN ATTORNEY-CLIENT RELATIONSHIP. YOU SHOULD NOT ACT OR RELY UPON THE INFORMATION IN THIS REPORT WITHOUT SEEKING THE ADVICE OF AN ATTORNEY BECAUSE CHANGES IN THE LAW OCCUR FREQUENTLY AND YOU SHOULD CONSULT WITH AN ATTORNEY WITH RESPECT TO YOUR PARTICULAR SITUATION. ADVERTISING MATERIAL: THE CHOICE OF A LAWYER IS AN IMPORTANT DECISION AND SHOULD NOT BE BASED SOLELY ON ADVERTISEMENTS. PAST RESULTS AFFORD NO GUARANTEE OF FUTURE RESULTS. EACH CASE IS DIFFERENT AND IS JUDGED ON ITS OWN MERITS.

Read Inside to Learn What Insurance Companies Don't Want You to Know About Your Injury Claim.

If you or someone you love has recently been injured in an accident, you may have questions like:

- What will the insurance company offer me for my injuries?
- How will I know if the insurance company's settlement offer is fair?
- Should I hire an attorney to represent me, and if so, how do I find the right one?
- Should I give a recorded statement to the insurance adjuster or sign their forms?
- Who will pay my medical bills?
- Will I be paid for the time I'm losing from work?
- What do I do if the person who hit my car doesn't have car insurance?

If you or someone you care about has any of these concerns, this book is for you. Please keep reading, and if you have questions or would like to speak with our firm about your claim, please call 816-203-0143. We would love to hear from you, and your question or issue may help us improve future versions of this book.

Table of Contents

Forward: Who Wrote This Book and Why?

Dear Reader:

I wrote this book to help people who have been injured in accidents in Missouri and Kansas. If you or a loved one have been injured in an accident, you probably have a lot of questions. The insurance company may be calling and asking you to sign their forms. They may have even offered you money. You may be wondering if you need an attorney.

This book is for you. It will give you the inside information you need ***before*** you talk to the adjuster, sign any forms or hire an attorney. You may not even need to hire an attorney, but please read this book before you do anything else.

For many years, I have represented individuals in Missouri and Kansas who have been injured in accidents. Early in my career, I worked at a "big firm" and represented insurance companies. Through that experience, I learned the inner workings of how big insurance companies deny claims and make money. It was not a good fit for me, but it taught me how insurance companies and their attorneys evaluate cases and avoid paying claims.

I am inspired everyday by my clients' stories, whether it's the executive who returns to work despite functional deficits, the teenage girl who sees her scars as badges of courage, the laborer who starts a new trade due to limitations from a car crash. Our firm exists to help our clients succeed despite tremendous challenges. This book shares some of the lessons we have learned along the way. My hope is that it will be helpful to you and others who may be struggling with similar issues.

If you have any questions about this book or a specific legal issue, please feel free to call our office. Please feel free to look to us for help when you need it. We would be excited to serve you.

Sincerely,

Kevin McManus

www.KevinMcManusLaw.com

About Kevin McManus:

- Attorney representing individuals injured in accidents
- Named "Best of the Bar" by *Kansas City Business Journal*
- Recognized by *SuperLawyers* Magazine as a "Rising Star"
- Licensed in Kansas and Missouri with active trial practices in both states
- Graduate of Roberts Trial Academy, Kansas City Metropolitan Bar Association
- Member of City Council in Kansas City, Missouri, with extensive knowledge and experience in transportation laws
- Former member of the Missouri House of Representatives and recipient of legislative award from the Missouri Bar for contributions to civil justice issues
- Author of numerous consumer books and reports

How Is Our Law Firm Different?

We are different from most law firms. We know all our clients by their name. Our purpose is simple—to help our clients achieve their highest potential in spite of whatever challenges they face. We believe we can best do that when we know our clients as people and not just as numbers.

This philosophy and set of values guide how we do our work and the experience you will have if you hire our firm. Our goal is not to be the biggest law firm in the state. We do not rely on a high volume of cases. We do not advertise on television or in the yellow pages. We do not claim to handle every kind of legal case. We do not want to do every kind of case, and frankly, we do not need to.

We only accept a limited number of serious injury and accident cases each year. Unlike some "injury mill" firms, we do not accept cases with questionable merit or try to settle large numbers of cases for pennies on the dollar. Our paralegals and assistants do not negotiate cases with the insurance company. By limiting our practice and taking fewer cases, we are able to give each of our clients the attention and care that they deserve, and we believe this produces better results.

We take pride in our results-driven, client-centered approach. Communication with our clients is a critical part of this. We will explain the legal process to you, answer all your questions, and keep you informed about your case.

Sometimes the advice you receive when you are considering a lawsuit is that you do not have a claim that can be won. If that is true, we will tell you. We will also tell you if we think that you are better off handling your claim without an attorney.

But, if we are your attorney, you can rest assured that you will receive our personal attention. We will aggressively represent you, keep you advised on the progress of your case, and give you straight advice on whether you should settle or go to trial.

Together, we will act as a team to decide on the best strategy to resolve your case.

8 Myths About Injury Cases

- The insurance company for the party that caused the accident cares about you and wants to help you.
- If you are reasonable with the insurance company, they will be reasonable and fair with you in return.
- If the accident wasn't your fault, the insurance company for the "at fault" party must pay your medical bills and lost wages as they are incurred.
- If the insurance company asks for a recorded statement, you must give it to them or they will not make you a settlement offer.
- Any attorney can handle an injury claim with the same level of skill and competence, especially if they advertise.
- Your lawyer should refer you to doctors and that will help your case.
- There is a mathematical formula for calculating a fair settlement.
- Juries in Missouri and Kansas always side with the person who was injured and are very generous.

This Book Dispels These Myths and Gives You Inside Information for Your Injury Claim!

What Is a Personal Injury Case?

Let's start at the beginning: what is a personal injury case? When attorneys say that they handle "personal injury" or "wrongful death" cases, what does that mean? A personal injury case is any type of claim where a person has been injured due to someone else's carelessness, recklessness or intentional act. In these circumstances, an injured person may make a legal claim to recover compensation for injuries and other damages caused by the other party. Personal injury claims can result from a car, truck or motorcycle accident, dangerous property condition, defective product, dog bite — the possibilities are endless.

If someone's carelessness or recklessness causes the death of a person, a "wrongful death" claim arises. The law of each state or jurisdiction differs significantly regarding what can be recovered in a wrongful death case. You need an attorney who understands the particular wrongful death laws that apply.

If you were in a car accident and the only damage was to your car, you do not have a personal injury claim, but you may have a property damage case. Our firm does not handle cases with no injuries and only property damage, but there are attorneys who do. If you were injured and your car was damaged, then you have both a personal injury and a property damage claim. Your insurance company (if you have collision coverage) or the other driver's insurance company may pay your property damage claim. Your personal injury claim is often a more complicated legal matter.

After an accident, the most important thing is to seek prompt medical treatment for your injuries. As you progress in your recovery, you also need to be thinking about how to protect your legal rights.

Unfortunately, many injury victims do not think about this until it is too late. They may not properly document what happened, conduct an investigation into the cause of the accident, or take the steps necessary to pursue a settlement or file a lawsuit. It is important to understand that you are not entitled to money just because you were hurt. You have to prove certain things to be legally entitled to compensation.

What Must You Prove to Win?

To win your case, you must prove that your injuries and damages were caused by someone else's carelessness or recklessness. If you have been injured in an accident and no one was at fault, then you will lose your case, and you will not recover any money. If you sue the wrong person, or if you wait too long to sue, you will also lose your case. If you already had an injury before the accident, you are only entitled to compensation to the extent your injury was made worse by the accident. This is sometimes difficult to prove. If you were partially at fault for the accident, you may not be able to recover anything, or your recovery may be reduced by the amount you were at fault, depending on the state law that applies and how much you were at fault.

Our experience in dealing with personal injury and wrongful death cases has taught us that accidents can happen in many different ways and for many different reasons. By handling a wide variety of injury cases, we know how critical it is to conduct an immediate investigation and take certain steps to protect your claim. This may include hiring expert investigators, forensic experts, engineers or other professionals necessary to prove your claim. Our firm advances these costs for our personal injury clients so they do not have to incur that expense. We also help develop and implement a strategy to maximize your recovery so you can focus on what is most important — getting better.

You are going to battle–
but with the right plan, it can be won.

You may not realize it yet, but your injury has put you in a war zone. Insurance companies, special interest groups and some in government have declared war on injured people and their attorneys. They are waging war in Congress and state legislatures across the country. Their purpose is to make it harder for injury victims to be treated fairly and to maximize profits for the insurance industry. This is no exaggeration — I served as a member of the Missouri legislature for five years and saw it firsthand.

Right now, an army of insurance lobbyists are working day and night (don't worry — they are paid well!) to write and pass laws to make it harder for you to receive fair compensation. These laws are often referred to as "tort reform." This is not a fair fight — injured people don't hire lobbyists!

This war is also being waged in the media through propaganda and public relations efforts with the goal of negatively influencing juries and their verdicts in personal injury lawsuits.

These efforts have shifted enormous power and leverage to insurance companies, which directly impacts how insurance companies will treat your case. Insurance companies often refuse to make a fair offer of settlement until you prove to them that you are ready and able to go to trial.

A Few Words About Insurance Companies

Many of our clients are surprised when they learn that insurance companies and their claim agents are not their friends. Clients are shocked to find out that some insurance companies will deny a claim even if they know their insured is at fault. I'm often asked by clients: "Why would they do that?"

The insurance adjusters know they can deny some claims, and if people are not aware of their rights or willing to fight back, millions (perhaps even billions) of dollars will be added to the bottom-line of the insurance company.

If you talk with the opposing insurance adjuster on your own, they will use different tactics to get you to settle your case before talking with a lawyer. Some of those tactics include:

1. **Acting Like They Are Your Friend and Pretending They Care.**

I had a client recently tell me that she thought the

insurance company was more pleasant before our firm was hired. I'm sure they were! They were real nice until they offered to reimburse her for a small fraction of her medical bills, which is why she hired us. After we got involved, she received more than enough to pay her bills and to cover her pain and suffering.

Let me again state the obvious — the insurance adjuster for the at-fault party is not your friend. They do not care about you. They want this claim closed for the smallest amount possible. This is a tactic to stop you from hiring an attorney and getting the legal advice that you need to ensure a fair recovery.

2. Arguing About Your Medical Treatment.

Insurance adjusters suddenly become medical experts when they talk to you on the phone about your accident. Of course, the treatment the adjuster "recommends" is much, much less than what your doctor suggests. They may try to make you feel guilty for seeking the medical care recommended by your doctor because "most people are better by now." Remember — the insurance adjuster is not your doctor.

3. Disputing Medical Charges.

Insurance adjusters will complain about the cost of medical treatment and that the hospital bills are too high. Everyone agrees that medical care is too expensive, but that is not your fault. You were injured by their insured! You should not be penalized because the care was expensive — that is why people buy insurance. Just imagine how much the insurance adjuster saves if he is able to get everybody to accept a 25% discount.

4. Delay, Delay and More Delay.

The insurance company knows you have missed work (and may still be missing work) and that your bills for deductibles and medical care are growing every day. The more delay by the insurance company, the more pressure on you to settle for cash. They are well aware of this financial leverage, and they will use it to get you to settle your case for much less than you deserve.

5. Requesting Meaningless Information.

By making you find every little piece of information,

even if it ultimately does nothing to your claim, insurance companies add unnecessary delay to your case and continue to earn interest on the money they are not paying you.

6. Misrepresenting Available Insurance

Some insurance companies will flat-out lie to you about the amount of insurance available. In certain circumstances, insurance policies and coverage can be "stacked," so there may be more insurance available than you think. If you knew that, you would fight harder. Be careful!

Do You Need an Attorney?

An attorney is not needed for every small injury case. Our office will not accept your case if there is little or no property damage or if your injuries are very minor. Why not? If your damages are small, you may be left with very little to pay your medical bills after the attorney fee and costs are deducted. This would not be fair to you. However, Missourians and Kansans who have serious injuries should consider having someone on their side.

WARNING: TIME MAY BE RUNNING OUT!

The law imposes strict deadlines to file suit, provide notice and assert claims for different types of actions. These time limitations can be short and vary greatly depending on what law and jurisdiction applies. The failure to act timely can destroy your claim and right to compensation. For this reason, it is critical that you speak with an experienced attorney as soon as you can.

What Are the Benefits of Hiring an Attorney?

There are many benefits to hiring an attorney to represent you in your personal injury case, including:

- Having someone on your side fighting for you, protecting your rights and explaining how the legal system works.
- Eliminating the stress of dealing with the insurance company and ensuring that you receive the fair and full value of your case.
- Removing the pressure of collection agencies and medical providers calling you about medical bills because they will be directed to contact us.
- Maximizing your recovery by negotiating and reducing liens or claims for payment being asserted by hospitals, medical providers, Medicare, Medicaid, etc.
- Ensuring that your case is prepared and ready for trial if it cannot be settled.

How Do I Find a Qualified Injury Attorney?

Hiring an attorney to represent you is a very important task but can be quite overwhelming and confusing. Your decision should not be made on the basis of advertising alone. Television, the internet and Yellow Pages are filled with attorney advertisements that basically say the same thing. You should not hire an attorney solely based upon these advertisements.

How do you find the right attorney for your case? There are specific questions you should ask to find the best attorney for your particular case.

Personal injury cases should be handled by someone who regularly practices personal injury law. Too often, we have looked at cases that inexperienced attorneys previously handled. The insurance companies know which attorneys actually go to court and try cases and who just settles. The insurance companies use this information to evaluate their risk and minimize the amount they offer and pay.

Here are some tips for finding the right attorney in your area:

1. Get a referral from an attorney you know. He or she may know someone who focuses in the area of law that you need. If you need an attorney in an area that we do not handle, call us. We can help you find the right attorney for your case.
2. Before you visit with an attorney, see if he or she has information like this book available or a website that details his or her qualifications, experience, results and verdicts, what past clients have to say, and the methods used in handling a case.
3. The Internet or Yellow Pages can be a good source of names. However, please keep in mind the following: (i) advertisements are not a substitute for experience and reputation (most of our cases are from referrals by other attorneys and satisfied clients); (ii) be careful about attorney advertisements that claim many different specialties (for example, family law, criminal law, personal injury, trusts and estates) because no one can do everything well; (iii) advertisements typically attract

a lot of cases, including the small cases of questionable quality, so be sure the attorney you hire is selective and able to give your case the attention it deserves.

4. Be careful about any attorney who rushes you to sign a contingent fee agreement. Make sure you read and understand this document. Also, beware of an attorney who immediately wants to send you to one of his or her doctors.
5. Ask your attorney if he or she is licensed in the state where your case will be filed and whether he or she has ever been disciplined by a state bar.
6. Avoid any attorney who calls you first or who is associated with a "runner" — a person who "runs" to a hospital, accident scene or your house to pressure you to sign a fee agreement.
7. Here are factors to ask a potential attorney about:
    a. Experience: How long has the attorney been practicing? Does he or she concentrate his or her practice on personal injury cases in the state where you were injured? Does the attorney have a record of successfully resolving a case like yours?

b. Reputation and respect in the legal community: Is the attorney known and respected in the legal community? Has he or she been recognized or received any awards from *Superlawyers,* business journals, or the state bar association?
c. Publications: Has your attorney written anything that has been published and was it on a subject relevant to your case?
d. Continuing Education: Does the attorney speak at continuing legal education seminars to other lawyers?
e. Membership in trial lawyer associations: Is the attorney a member of the Missouri Association of Trial Attorneys, Kansas Trial Lawyers Association, or American Association for Justice? These organizations offer a variety of education and networking opportunities for trial lawyers.
f. Client satisfaction: Ask the attorney to show you what past clients have to say about their experience.
g. Attorney Rating: Does the attorney have a rating of "9.0" or above on the attorney

rating site www.Avvo.com? This rating is considered "superb" and is based on a combination of education, experience, and what other attorneys and clients have said about the attorney.

h. Communication and Personal Attention: Ask the attorney who will be handling your case how he or she will keep you informed about your case and whether the firm has sufficient time to take your case. If you are hiring an attorney for his or her trial skills, you want to make sure that attorney will be handling the important aspects of your case.

What Does an Experienced Injury Attorney Do?

Below is a list of the actions our firm takes with most injury cases. Please keep in mind that each case is different, and not all of these actions are required in every case.

- Initial interview with the client
- Educate our client about applicable personal injury laws and court rules
- Review and analyze the client's insurance policies to see what coverage is available to pay all or a portion of the medical bills while the claim is pending
- Gather documentary evidence, including police accident reports, medical records, films and bills
- Hire an investigator, as needed, to interview witnesses, locate witnesses, etc.
- Collect other evidence, such as photographs of the vehicles and accident scene

- Review and analyze the client's health insurance policy or other benefits plan to ascertain whether any money he or she spent to pay medical bills must be repaid
- Review and analyze all legal issues, such as comparative fault and assumption of the risk
- Provide the client a fair, unbiased opinion as to the merits of the case and the likelihood of winning
- Talk to the client's physicians or obtain written reports from them to understand the client's prognosis
- Review and analyze the validity of any liens on the case that doctors, insurance companies, welfare benefit plans and employers may assert relating to the client's recovery
- Contact the insurance company to put them on notice of the claim
- Decide with the client whether an attempt will be made to negotiate the case with the

insurance company or whether suit shall be filed

- If suit is filed, prepare the client, witnesses and health care providers for depositions
- Prepare and respond to written discovery, which includes requests for documents and written questions and answers from the defendant
- Prepare and take the deposition of the defendant and other witnesses
- Produce to the defendant all of the pertinent data for the claim, such as medical bills, medical records, etc.
- Conduct a scheduling conference to set a trial date
- Prepare a demand package to send to the defendant in attempt to settle the case
- Prepare for a possible mediation and/or settlement before trial
- Prepare for trial, including preparing the client and witnesses

- Organize and prepare medical exhibits for trial
- Organize and prepare demonstrative exhibits for trial
- File motions with the court to determine what evidence will be allowed at trial
- Take the case to trial with a jury
- Review and analyze the verdict to determine if either side has good grounds to appeal the case
- Make any recommendations to the client after the verdict

Who Should Pay for My Medical Bills?

In accident cases in Missouri and Kansas, it is rare for the other party's insurance company to make payments directly to your medical providers for your bills. This is true even if liability is obvious and they have already paid for your property damage. The other driver's insurance company typically only makes a payment at the time of a final settlement when they can obtain a signed release of liability from you.

As a result, you should not expect that the other driver's insurance company will pay your medical bills as they are incurred. You should look to one of the following means to obtain payment of your medical bills (please keep in mind that an attorney can assist you in choosing the best method to pay your medical expenses):

1. Your own health insurance from your place of employment.
2. Your own health insurance that you paid for personally.

3. Health insurance obtained by your spouse for your benefit or by your parents if you are under age.
4. Medical payments or personal injury protection insurance coverage from your own insurance policy if you were driving your automobile or were a passenger in a vehicle. Sometimes, you can receive this coverage from the insurance company for the vehicle you were in as well as your own insurance company if you were not in your own vehicle.
5. Medicaid / Medicare / Tricare / www.Healthcare.gov. If you are not covered under an insurance plan you may be eligible for one of these government sponsored insurance programs. You should contact your local Department of Human Services to find out. If you qualify for one of these programs, it is very that you notify our firm. We will need to ensure that their lien is

identified and timely submitted for repayment as required by law.

6. Your own personal funds if you were not insured and are able to pay medical bills as they are incurred.

If there are insufficient funds to pay doctors, hospitals, and other medical bills, our office will help facilitate liens whereby the client authorizes our office to pay the medical provider directly from any settlement or verdict. These often will serve to satisfy the health provider, and they often will wait until the time of settlement rather than pursue collection against you.

Keep in mind that some insurance policies have a subrogation provision. This means they will require reimbursement from you if you obtain money for your medical bills from another party or insurance company. Subrogation is discussed in more detail below.

What is Subrogation?

Subrogation is the process in which an insurance company seeks reimbursement for what they have paid. Subrogation can be pursued by certain health insurance plans for medical bills paid on your behalf in an accident. Subrogation rights vary based on what state or federal law applies. For example, in Kansas, your car insurance company may use subrogation to seek reimbursement for medical expenses they paid under your personal injury protection coverage. As a result, it is important to take into consideration the amount of money that you will have to pay back from any proceeds you receive. Also, in certain cases, a federal law called ERISA may apply as described below. An experienced personal injury attorney can explain the subrogation process in more detail and help you through it.

Watch Out for ERISA Subrogation

You should be aware that, if your medical bills were paid by health insurance of an employer's health plan, the insurance company or plan may want you to reimburse it out of any personal injury recovery. The laws in some states, including Missouri and Kansas, generally prohibit such claims, but they may try to seek reimbursement regardless. This area of law, known as "reimbursement" or "subrogation" can be very complicated and is sometimes governed by a federal law called ERISA (The Employee Retirement Income Security Act of 1974). Your attorney must understand the implications of ERISA on your case.

There are other liens that may affect what you ultimately get paid in your case. If your bills were paid by Medicare, Medicaid, or Tricare, you may be forced to pay back a portion of your settlement as reimbursement for costs paid by government sponsored health insurance. We routinely help our clients navigate these complex issues and reduce these liens to the extent legally possible.

Who Will Pay My Lost Wages?

It is rare in an accident case that the insurance company for the other party will pay your lost wages as you incur them. Generally, you have to rely on one or more of the following as an income source if you are not able to work after an accident:

1. Short term/long term disability insurance you may have through work or purchased on your own.
2. Accident and disability policies you have through work or purchased on your own.
3. Your own personal funds or borrowing money from family or friends until you can pay them back from the money from your case.

Can My Employer Fire Me?

This is a question we hear from many clients with serious injuries. Unfortunately, the general answer is "Yes". Both Missouri and Kansas are employee-at-will states. This means that your employer can fire you for any reason or no reason at all so long as they do not violate anti-discrimination laws or other applicable state or federal laws.

For example, there are some federal laws such as the FMLA (the Family Medical Leave Act) and ADA (American with Disabilities Act). These laws provide some protection in narrow circumstances. In addition, if you have an employment contract or are a member of a union subject to a collective bargaining agreement, then you may have additional protection such as filing a grievance. If you are wrongfully terminated, any claim that arises would be a separate employment law case.

What Damages Can I Recover?

If your injuries were caused by someone else's carelessness or negligence, state law entitles you to recover various types of damages, including:

Medical Expenses: You are entitled to recover the cost of all reasonable and necessary medical expenses incurred and those that are reasonably certain to be incurred in the future because of your injury. These expenses include past (already-incurred) medical expenses and also future medical expenses, which may be caused by the original injury or that result from an increased susceptibility to future injury. There will likely be disagreement on what is included and how to calculate this figure. However, all forms of care and treatment, whether hospital, medical, therapy, nursing, diagnostic testing, surgery, physical rehabilitation or pain management are included.

Lost Wages: You are also entitled to recover your lost wages caused by your injuries. For persons who are hourly or salaried employees, this can be calculated based on your pay scale and work time lost due to your injuries. For self-employed individuals, it can be more difficult to calculate this figure, but we can use prior earnings history to support the amount lost.

Loss of Earnings Capacity: If your injuries permanently limit your ability to earn, you can recover the value of the reduction in earning capacity if there is reasonable probability that you will have a loss in earning capacity in the future. These damages compensate you for your lost earning power over the remainder of your working years.

Pain and Suffering: This is compensation for loss of quality of life including physical pain and mental anguish you have suffered and will endure in the future because of your injury. These general damages are in addition to and may be more than the amount of your lost earnings and medical expenses.

Scarring or Disfigurement: If the injury causes scarring or other permanent disfigurement, you may be entitled to damages for that condition.

Damaged Property. This can include damages to your car or home, if it was damaged in the accident.

Punitive Damages. In certain circumstances, courts have awarded punitive damages to victims of personal injury. These damages are meant to punish the guilty party for his or her actions beyond what the court deems the victim should receive for his or her losses.

Death: Damages for "wrongful death" are usually available to the beneficiaries (often the wife, husband, parent or child) of the deceased person. Damages are not limited to economic loss and may include damages for loss of consortium which the law defines as loss of companionship, comfort, guidance, affection, general usefulness, industry and attention within the home and family. Damages are also available for the deceased's lost accumulation of value to his/her estate and pre-death pain and suffering.

How Much is My Case Worth?

This is a question we often hear from clients during our initial interview. Every case is different, and we cannot tell you how much your case is worth until we have all the facts. Be careful of attorneys who tell you that your case is worth a certain amount before knowing all the facts. It is a dangerous practice and can cause problems when it is time to try to settle your case. Sometimes doctors will change their opinions, factual witnesses are not able to be found, etc.

Your own liability in the accident will come into play when it comes to calculating what your case may be worth. If the court determines that you were, say, 25 percent liable for your accident, your award could be reduced by that amount. This is an area where different states have varying laws. For example, in Kansas, if you are found to be 50 percent liable or more, Kansas law bars you from recovering anything at all.

For this reason, it is important to do a thorough investigation and case analysis to value the case properly. After we have gathered all the facts, conducted discovery, spoken with your doctors, and prepared a demand package, then we will be able to discuss the value of your case.

Another factor that is critical in determining case value is the amount of insurance the at-fault party has to pay for your damages. This is important because, if the other party has no insurance or too little insurance, your ability to recover may be severely limited. This issue often arises in the context of car accident cases.

What happens in a car accident if the other driver has no insurance?

If the other driver did not have insurance, then you may have coverage under your own insurance policy to pay for your damages. Missouri and Kansas law require that every driver have a car insurance policy that includes what is called "uninsured motorists' coverage." If you or a loved one is injured by someone without insurance, then you should review your insurance policy to determine the amount of coverage that you have. One resource you should review is my other book, *Buying Car Insurance,* which will show you how to confirm the amount of coverage you have. It also provides a lot more information on this subject. If you would like a free copy of this book, please contact me. There is a form at the end of this book that you can use to request a copy.

What happens in a car accident if the other driver does not have enough insurance?

If the other driver had insurance but does not have enough to cover your bills and damages, then you should check to see if you have "under-insured motorist coverage" in your own policy. If you do, your insurance company may cover the difference between what the other party has to pay and what you are owed.

Missouri law does not require drivers to carry "under-insured motorist coverage". Kansas requires its drivers to carry a small amount. Regardless, we recommend that our clients buy as much uninsured and under-insured coverage as they can afford because for a small additional price you can receive a lot of additional protection for you and your family. Again, if you would like more information about this subject, use the form at the end of this book to request a free copy of *Buying Car Insurance.* I would be happy to send it to you.

What is the Legal Process for an Injury Case?

After investigating the accident and reviewing all your medical records, your attorney should have a strategy to resolve your claim with the insurance company. Your attorney will help you evaluate your case and the insurance company's best offer and compare it to what you may expect at trial after deducting the additional costs and expenses for trying the case. He or she should also explain to you that juries are unpredictable, and any case can be lost at trial, even if the case is seemingly clear cut.

Many times, negotiation with the insurance company before filing suit is not worth the effort. Insurance companies often use the pre-suit negotiation only to attempt to find out as much about you, your attorney and your doctor as they can. Many attorneys waste precious time attempting to negotiate with the insurance company before filing suit. If we accept your case it is because we believe that it has legal merit and that you deserve a trial if we are not able to reach a settlement.

It is a dangerous practice to wait until the last minute before the statute of limitations expires to file suit. We have seen other attorneys do this only to find that the defendant they sued is either not the correct defendant or is now blaming someone else. This can ruin the case.

While there can be legitimate reasons for waiting to file suit, an attorney should not wait until the last minute with the hope that the insurance company will settle your case. Unfortunately, we have seen attorneys not licensed in Missouri or Kansas attempt to represent people with claims in those jurisdictions. When the claims do not settle, they try to find an attorney to file the case on time. This is one reason why it is dangerous for a client to hire an attorney who is not licensed in the jurisdiction where the suit must be filed.

Once the lawsuit is filed, both sides begin what is called "discovery." Discovery is the process in which both sides attempt to discover what the evidence will be and what the other side will present at trial. The defendant will be allowed to review your medical records, work records and income tax returns. You may be required to give a deposition under oath and/or submit to a medical examination by a doctor hired by the defendant. We are also allowed to conduct discovery upon the defendant. The defendant will have to answer written questions called interrogatories, produce documents and be required to answer questions under oath in a deposition.

9 Mistakes That Can Wreck Your Injury Case

After being injured in an accident, most people are in a complete state of shock. Once that wears off, adrenaline kicks in, and it becomes easier to operate in the moment without considering the long-term effects on one's actions.

Since you aren't immediately thinking about filing a lawsuit, it's easy to make mistakes at the accident scene that may dramatically affect a future lawsuit. Other mistakes can be made later on due to inexperience or lack of knowledge as to how the legal system works. I hope that by reading this book, you will have the tools you need to avoid making the following nine mistakes that can wreck your injury claim.

Mistake #1: Failing to Document the Accident at the Scene

After an accident, it is easy to forget to document and preserve evidence of what happened. First, if you are injured, call 911 and request an ambulance.

If it is an accident involving a car, truck or motorcycle, you should ask for the police to be dispatched too, even if no one is injured. Police serve two purposes. First, they ensure the safety of those involved in the crash and others who are using the roadway. Second, they will create a police report that documents what happened and who was involved in the accident. This report will be important in your legal case.

You should not simply rely on the police to get all the necessary information. You should also document where the accident occurred, the license plate numbers of the vehicles involved, and the names and insurance companies for the parties. You should obtain the names, contact information and statements of any witnesses. You can use the camera on your phone to take pictures of the scene, the vehicles involved and any injuries you or others have suffered. If there was a dangerous condition in the roadway that caused the crash, take a picture or video of it with your phone. Pictures and videos are valuable pieces of evidence that will be useful later on.

Mistake #2: Failing to Get Prompt Medical Treatment

If you are seriously injured, you will likely be taken to a hospital by ambulance. However, in some accidents, you may believe you suffered only minor injuries and think you can tough it out without medical treatment.

Please do not do this. By delaying treatment, you are taking a big risk with your health and your legal case. Some injuries do not show up immediately but can be very serious. You may have internal bleeding but not show any external sign of injury. Delay in this situation can be deadly. Your neck or back pain at the accident scene may not feel that intense, but weeks or even months later, you may find out that you have a herniated disc, the pain is unbearable and you require surgery. The point is this – just because an injury is not immediately evident does not mean it is not serious.

Please get prompt treatment so a medical professional can evaluate, diagnose and treat your injuries properly and without delay. This can literally save your life. In addition, the longer you wait to get medical attention, the more difficult it can be to prove your injuries were caused by the accident.

Mistake #3: Not Following Your Doctor's Advice or Missing Appointments

You will damage your claim if your doctor tells you to go physical therapy three days a week and you only go once a week. The insurance company will assume that you were not really injured because you did not follow your doctor's recommendations. This will result in a reduced settlement offer to you.

In addition, if you do not see your physician regularly, the insurance company will argue that you are fully recovered. While you should not go to the doctor every day, you need to see your doctors and tell them if you are still having problems. If your doctor says "follow up as needed," you need to go back in a few weeks if you are still having problems. If you do not follow up, the doctor, insurance company, and likely a jury will believe you have made a full recovery.

Mistake #4: Exaggerating Your Injuries or Hiding Prior Injuries

Some people think they can increase the settlement value if they exaggerate the extent of their injuries or if they hide a prior injury. This is a big mistake — the opposite is true. When you make an insurance claim, your medical history is an open book. You should also be aware that insurance defense lawyers can and do obtain surveillance videos of claimants.

If there is a medical record or — even worse, a surveillance video — that contradicts your testimony about the extent of your injuries or your prior medical condition, the insurance company will use it to destroy your credibility and case. This is a simple rule — be honest. Tell the truth. Obviously, you should be open and honest very early on with your attorney about your injuries and medical history so he or she can properly evaluate your case.

Mistake #5: Failing to Report Your Symptoms or Pain

While you should not exaggerate your injuries, you also should not downplay them. A common mistake injured people make is failing to give an accurate report of their pain or injuries during a medical exam.

Your medical visits usually start the same way — the nurse and then doctor ask you a series of questions about your pain and injuries. It may feel routine, but your answers are important. Many people do not give their answers the thought and attention they deserve.

If the doctor comes in and asks, "how you are doing?," you may simply reply, "I'm doing okay" or "Fine, how are you doing?" This seemingly innocuous reply may be documented later in your medical records as "the patient says she is doing well today." That may not be accurate as to how you feel. However, once it appears in your medical records, it will be hard to convince a jury otherwise.

You need to be careful when you describe your pain

and injuries. Describe them to your doctor completely and with specificity. Tell the doctor every single area of pain you have that is related to the car wreck. If your neck hurts really bad, you may be tempted to talk about just that and not mention your foot and wrist pain. Do not do that! It is important not to exaggerate your injuries but also not to discount or ignore them. Be honest, open and detailed when talking to your physician.

Mistake #6: Signing Documents or Giving Recorded Statements to the Opposing Insurance Adjuster

Insurance companies train their adjusters to be courteous and pleasant, but you need to be very careful when you speak to them. Their job is to get information that they can later use against you and your case.

What should you do when the adjuster for the other driver's insurance company calls you? The simplest response is to tell them to talk to your lawyer. If you do not have a lawyer yet, the adjuster will often ask you to give them a recorded statement about the accident. They may even tell you that they cannot pay you anything until you give a recorded statement. This is not true. You do not have to give them a recorded statement.

Instead, you should focus on getting better. When you are ready, you can get a free consultation from an attorney or review free information like this book, so you are ready to move forward with your claim.

Mistake #7: Failing to Keep Accurate Tax Records

To prove the amount of your lost income caused by the accident, you must prove what your income was before you were injured, and tax returns are used for this purpose. As a result, your tax records will be provided to the insurance company if you are seeking to recover lost income due to the accident. If your tax returns show any misrepresentation of your income, it will not only damage your credibility and case, but it will also expose you to criminal liability. You need to be up front with your attorney so they can be prepared for any issue. Our firm does not handle criminal cases, and we will not represent anyone who cheats on their taxes.

Mistake #8: Delaying and Missing the Statute of Limitations

Statutes of limitations are laws that dictate deadlines for filing suit. These laws vary by state and the type of claim. If you fail to file your lawsuit before the statute of limitations expires, you are forever barred from filing your case. Once that deadline passes, the insurance company will not pay you any money.

This is an incredibly important area of law, and accurate information is critical. Do not ever guess about a statute of limitations or rely on what you've heard from any source other than a lawyer who knows the statutes of limitations that apply in your case.

Speed is important to protect your legal rights. You should seek and receive objective advice about your accident in a timely manner. Otherwise, you may be denied justice and compensation. Our firm has never been contacted too early about a potential claim, but there are claimants who are too late.

Mistake #9: Failing to Consult with an Attorney or to Educate Yourself

You may not need to *hire* an attorney, but you should consider *consulting* with one. As mentioned earlier, some simple cases with minor injuries may be settled without an attorney. Most personal injury attorneys will provide you with a free consultation. Our firm provides free consultations but also goes a step further by giving you free, high-quality information to help educate you about your legal rights and claim. We do this to help those who have been injured through no fault of their own and because we believe that well-educated clients are our best clients. By reading this book, you are already taking action so you do not make this mistake!

Why Should You Consider Hiring Our Firm?

As I said at the beginning of this book, we are not your typical law firm. Instead of trying to manage hundreds of cases at a time, we carefully select the few cases that we will accept at any one time.

There are many attorneys who advertise for personal injury cases. Unfortunately, some of these attorneys have so many small cases in their offices that no case gets their personal attention. Others have no real intention of trying your case themselves, and if the case cannot be settled with the insurance company, they will refer the case out for trial. Many will not even try to talk with your doctors until they ask for their opinions for the first time during a deposition. There are good experienced attorneys in this field, but it can be very difficult for a consumer to separate the good from the bad.

Our clients get personal attention because we are very selective in the cases that we take. We take the time and spend the money to go meet with your doctors and explain to them how they can assist in your case. We prepare every case like it is going to trial because we do not know which ones will need to be tried until the end.

What Cases Do We Generally Not Accept?

Due to the very high volume of calls and referrals from other attorneys that we receive, we have found that the only way to provide personal service is to decline those cases that do not meet our strict criteria. Therefore, we generally do not accept the following types of cases:

- Cases involving minor impact or minimal damages to the vehicle. Generally, this is defined as less than $500 in property damage to your car. Juries typically will not believe that minor impacts can cause substantial personal injury. We believe the risk and time spent by the client are too great and that our time is better spent helping those with other cases. There are other attorneys with different opinions about these cases, and we are happy to refer you to them.
- Cases where medical treatment is completed and there is less than $3,000 of total "hard

damages." Your case must have at least $3,000 in total past and future medical bills and/or past and future lost wages before we will consider accepting it. Please keep in mind this is not just out of pocket expenses such as co-pays and deductibles, these include the "total" medical charges.

- Cases with significant pre-existing injury in the same part of the body. For example, if you were treating with a doctor for a back injury at the time of your car accident and continue to have back problems after the accident, the chances of a jury awarding you substantial money for your back injuries is reduced.
- Cases where the statute of limitations is running out. We like to have at least three months to adequately investigate and evaluate your claim. Do not delay, and you will avoid this issue.
- Cases where you were found at fault and charged by the police in the accident.

- If your case has already been filed by another attorney, we will not represent you unless we have worked with that attorney previously. Our firm has our own process that we believe serves our clients best.

Are There Any Cases Left?

Yes, there are, and your case may be one. We represent many clients with significant claims. When we devote our time and resources to representing only legitimate claimants with good claims, we are able to do our best work. We have found that spending countless hours on lots of little cases, each with a "unique problem," is not good for our clients with legitimate claims.

Post-Accident: The Next Steps

It's tough for victims of personal injuries, even after they get out of the hospital and perhaps back to work, to think much beyond the immediate. How am I going to shop? Can I still pick up the kids? What about my last three missed paychecks? It's tough at times for personal injury victims to even contemplate the future.

While determining what the future holds may be too much for you to take in all at once, please consider taking some small but concrete steps one at a time.

- If you do not have an attorney, contact our office *before* you respond to any requests for information or sign any forms from insurance adjusters or investigators.
- Save all the information that comes your way—records, emails, notes, letters, statements and so on from doctors, hospitals, the ambulance company, etc. You will need these, and you don't want to rely on someone to resend a document by the time you might need it.

- Keep accurate records of all the time you have missed from work or had to take off because of doctors' appointments.
- Keep a journal of your medical, physical complications — aches, pains, anxiety, and dates, times, and places.
- Keep all your medical appointments and follow your doctors' and physical therapists' advice — failing to do so could make it look as though your injuries weren't as serious as they really were.
- If you ever need help in any of these matters, don't be shy or embarrassed — ask our office for help.

Conclusion

I hope this book is helpful in explaining the nine mistakes that can wreck your accident case, as well as the process for pursuing a personal injury claim if you or a loved one is injured by the negligence of others.

It is important to remember that, just as each person is unique, each case is different and unique. This book was not written to provide you with legal advice — only your attorney can do that. I wrote this book to give you a general understanding of what you can do if you are injured in a car accident or a loved one suffers catastrophic injuries or death as the result of the negligence of another.

If you believe we can help you with your case, please call us at (816) 203-0143. The call is free, and there is no cost to talk to an attorney about your case. If you want more information before calling our office, feel free to look at the information on our website at KevinMcManusLaw.com. You can learn more about our law firm, the cases we have handled, and additional information about accident cases in Missouri and Kansas.

Why Experience Matters

You should very concerned if an attorney guarantees a result based on a prior case he or she has handled. Each case is different, and past results are not a guarantee of future results. Nevertheless, when selecting an attorney, find an attorney with experience in personal injury cases. A brief story illustrates why.

In late 2017, we were contacted by a couple injured in a serious car accident in Johnson County, Kansas. The husband was driving, and his wife was riding in the front passenger seat. As he entered an intersection, another car ran a red light and struck them on the passenger side in a "T-bone" collision.

The husband was not very badly injured, but his wife was seriously injured because she was sitting where the impact occurred. She had multiple broken bones and a spinal injury. Surgery was required. Medical bills grew. They sought legal guidance.

They were referred to a criminal defense attorney

who supposedly did a little personal injury on the side. It is unclear what happened next, but nearly two years after the accident, they were referred to our firm. No lawsuit had been filed. No settlement offer had been made by the insurance company.

The statute of limitations for personal injury cases in Kansas is two years. This deadline is extremely important. If you do not assert all claims you have within two years, those claims are forever barred, and you will not recover a dime.

Our office pushes our cases forward so they are resolved as soon as possible. If they cannot be resolved with a pre-suit demand, we tell our client that we need to file suit, and we prepare for trial. Typically, we will not take a case if it is even close to the statute of limitations deadline.

We explained this to the couple, but they pleaded with our office to help. After reviewing the records, we discovered the reason why the insurance company was not paying them. There was no video of the crash. The husband said he had a green light, and the other driver said he had a green light. The insurance company was using their competing statements to deny paying the person who clearly was not at fault but who was most injured — the wife. She was not driving, but she was the one most badly injured. Even worse, they were saying the husband was at fault even though he was a retired professional driver with years of training and experience in safe driving.

After discussing various options and strategies with this couple, we agreed that we would represent only the wife and that we would file suit immediately against the other driver and the husband. Why? If the insurance company was going to argue that the husband was negligent, then we needed to add him as a defendant to force both insurance companies to the table. The husband and wife understood and agreed with this approach.

Within days of our filing suit and sending a demand, **BOTH** insurance companies – for the husband and the other driver – paid policy limits to our client. Each insurance company paid a six-figure amount, which in sum was well over her medical bills. Finally, the couple received fair compensation for the wife's pain and suffering.

The moral of the story is simple: experience matters. You need an attorney who has experience handling complex personal injury cases, who will investigate the facts fully and think creatively about strategies. The wrong decision can destroy your case and your right to recover compensation.

A Few of Our Case Results

Below is a sampling of cases that we have successfully resolved for clients in the past. Remember that each case is different. Once a case is in the hands of a jury, it is out of our control. However, we believe that significant trial experience in big cases is one factor that people may use to choose one attorney over another. With these things in mind, here are some of our results:

Policy Limits Settlement for Car Accident Victim Suffering Concussion

Our client was stopped at an intersection at the Country Club Plaza Shopping District in Kansas City, Missouri, when her vehicle was rear-ended by another driver. Our client's head hit the steering wheel of her vehicle on impact. She drove her vehicle from the scene to the emergency room after noticing symptoms of a head injury, including a headache, dizziness, confusion, disorientation, difficulty thinking and memory problems. She underwent a CT-Scan and testing and was diagnosed with a concussion without loss of consciousness, a mild form of traumatic brain injury. After our client completed physical and occupational therapy, we submitted a demand package with detailed information regarding traumatic brain injury (TBI), and the case was settled for policy limits.

Double Policy Limits for Client with Cervical Discectomy and Fusion Surgery

Our client's vehicle was struck by a truck exiting a gas station when she was stopped at an intersection at Blue Ridge Boulevard and Holmes Road in Kansas City, Missouri. Our client did not seek immediate medical treatment but noticed cervical pain and strain in the days following the accident. She went to her primary care physician who referred her to a neurosurgeon. She then underwent a MRI, which noted a herniated disc protruding 7mm at C3-C4 and flattening of the spinal cord at C3-4, C4-5, and C5-6 of her spine. It also confirmed multi-level cervical spinal canal stenosis with severe stenosis at C3-4, C4-5, and C5-6. Based on the exam and the imaging findings, our client's neurosurgeon recommended she undergo ACDF (anterior cervical discectomy and fusion) surgery from C3 to C6. The insurance company of the liable party paid policy limits within days after our demand package was submitted. Our firm then pursued the client's under-insurance policy to maximize the recovery for our client.

Double Recovery Against Deceased Drunk Driver

Our clients, a married couple, were stopped in their vehicle at a red light at the intersection of State Line Road and Red Bridge Road. While they were waiting for the light to turn green, their vehicle was struck violently from behind by another driver. Our clients both went to the emergency room for treatment and were diagnosed with neck and back strain / pain (Cervicalgia). Their injuries from the accident did not subside for months and required physical therapy and follow up medical care. After an investigation, we found the at-fault driver was issued a DUI at the scene and that he had been involved in another, second collision nearby. Unfortunately, our investigation also determined that this driver died after the crash from an unrelated cause. We preserved our client's claim by initiating suit and requesting the court to appoint a *defendant ad litem* to act on behalf of the deceased defendant. Ultimately, the insurance company agreed to settle the claims for both our clients in an amount far in excess of their past and future medical bills and lost wages.

Policy Limits for Client with Bulging Lumbar Discs

Our client was traveling westbound on Interstate 670 (I-670) just east of the Broadway Boulevard overpass in Kansas City, Missouri. Traffic slowed to an abrupt stop apparently due to congestion near the Broadway Boulevard exit ramp. Directly behind our client, another driver was traveling at a high rate of speed and failed to stop his vehicle in time. He collided his vehicle into the rear of the vehicle of our client, which totaled our client's car. Our client did not feel much pain until two days after the collision, which was the first time he sought medical care. He underwent CT scan, but no fractures were noted. Our client was recommended to physical therapy, which he was unable to complete due to worsening pain. An MRI was ordered which revealed multiple bulging lumbar discs in his spine along with spinal stenosis. Our client was recommended for injections and further physical therapy. The case settled for policy limits of the at-fault driver after our firm prepared and submitted a demand package.

Double Policy Limits Recovery for Passenger with Spine Injury

Our client was a passenger who was riding with her husband when their car was struck in a "T-bone" collision. The accident occurred in Johnson County, Kansas. There was no video evidence of how the collision occurred, and the drivers had conflicting accounts. Our client's husband said he had a green light at the intersection where the crash occurred and that the other car ran a red light before colliding on the passenger side where the wife was sitting. The other driver stated she had the green light. As a result, both insurance companies – for the husband and the other driver – were disputing liability and had refused to pay. However, our client was not at fault – she was simply riding as a passenger—and she was seriously injured with multiple broken bones, including a broken sacrum (the large, triangular bone at the base of the spine) that required surgery. After discussing with our client, we initiated suit against both the husband and other driver, and within days, both insurance companies paid full policy limits. The settlement more than covered our client's unpaid medical bills and provided her with the compensation she deserved for her painful injuries.

$527,000 Judgment for Dog Bite Victim

Our client was attacked by two vicious dogs when she was visiting her father's apartment residence in Wyandotte County, Kansas. The dogs were owned by the property owner who resided nearby and were known to have attacked other visitors and had allegedly killed another dog. Our client sustained severe bite injuries to her legs, hips and buttocks, which required surgery. Unfortunately, these injuries became infected, which required hospitalization and further treatment. We initiated suit, and after a hearing, the judgment was entered against the landowner in the amount of $527,000, which was roughly five times the amount of our client's medical bills.

$125,000 Trip & Fall Settlement Helps Client with Rare "Brittle Bone" Condition

Our client was a college student who suffered from a rare genetic disorder known as osteogenesis imperfecta ("OI"). OI is a disease characterized by the weakening of bones and is sometimes referred to as "brittle bone disease." This condition limited our client's mobility to a powered wheel-chair, which he controls. Our client was visiting an art museum with friends and was attempting to exit the building. As he moved his wheelchair through the doorway, his wheelchair hit an unmarked step that caused his wheelchair to topple over and his body to be thrown to the ground. Our client fractured his hip and right humerus (upper arm) bone. Due to the complex nature of his disease and injuries, two revision surgeries of previously implanted hardware were required. Our firm engaged an expert to investigate and opine as to the ADA and safety standards of the museum exit. After submission of a demand package, a six-figure settlement was reached. The settlement more than covered our client's past and future medical bills and will assist him in continuing his education. Our client plans to attend medical school and hopes to someday become a doctor specializing in helping patients who suffer from OI.

Day Care Shut Down After Child's Death (Confidential Settlement)

We initiated a wrongful death suit against a day care center in Wyandotte County, Kansas, on behalf of a mother of a young child who was found dead in a crib at the center. Our investigation found that the day care center had received multiple citations from the Kansas Department of Health and Environment (KSDHE), including citations for failure to follow safe sleep practices. After we filed suit, the KSDHE revoked the day care's license, and the center permanently closed its doors. The case was settled for a confidential amount shortly thereafter.

What Others Are Saying

Below are some testimonials from those we have worked with in the past. As you will discover, the issues you encounter do not have to be difficult, and help is available.

Kevin was very professional, but approachable and friendly. He kept me informed of the progress of my case and fought for me to receive the maximum I could receive. He finished my case in a few months, after I had been waiting for two years under another attorney.

-Kathleen, Johnson County, Kansas

Kevin McManus works hard for his clients and cares about his community. He represented me on a car accident case. Without his help, I would have been left with unpaid bills for my injuries and would never have received the compensation I deserved.

-Steve, Kansas City, Missouri

Kevin McManus is an excellent lawyer and a wonderful person. He cares about his clients and works very hard to obtain the very best results. I have worked with Kevin on several cases and have been very impressed with his work. Kevin is an absolute pleasure to work with, and he treats everyone like family.

-Scott Shachtman, Co-counsel

Kevin is a great lawyer who is very responsive. He is well-known in the community and can handle many different types of practice areas. I fully recommend him as an attorney.

-Phyllis Norman, Referring Attorney

FREE BOOK ON BUYING CAR INSURANCE

Great news! A free book is now available on how to buy car insurance to protect your family from irresponsible drivers in Missouri and Kansas. There is no obligation or cost with requesting this book. Our office is providing free copies to residents of Missouri and Kansas.

Copy and fill out this form and mail or e-mail this form back to us to learn:

- Who will pay my medical bills?
- Will I be paid for the time I'm losing from work?
- Should I give a recorded statement to the insurance adjuster or sign his or her forms?
- What do I do if the person who hit my car doesn't have car insurance?
- What if I don't make a full recovery and cannot return to work?
- How will I know if the insurance company's settlement offer is fair?

- Should I hire an attorney to represent me, and if so, how do I find the right one?

To receive this free book, just photocopy this form, fill it out and e-mail or mail it to us.

Email to:

InsuranceBook@KevinMcManusLaw.com or mail to Kevin McManus, 1100 Main Street, Suite 2620, Kansas City, MO 64105.

Please send me a free copy of: *Buying Car Insurance: A Complete Guide to Protecting Your Family from Irresponsible Drivers in Missouri & Kansas*

Name:

____

Address:

____

City:_______________ State: ___ Zip:______________

We do not share mail lists with anyone!

FREE INFORMATIONAL NEWSLETTERS

Want to know:

- How to best deal with insurance company denials?
- How to protect yourself from financial ruin?
- Legal insider tips about Kansas and Missouri law?
- How current legal issues and cases may affect you?
- Specific steps you can take to find the best lawyer for your case?
- Practical advice about buying insurance from one who does not sell insurance?

These are some of the topics that are covered monthly in our **free newsletter** that is available to you.

Our firm strongly believes that most legal disputes could be avoided if people had a better general knowledge about the legal system, insurance coverage, and the insurance claim process.

There is absolutely no cost or obligation to receive our newsletter, and from time to time, we run contests to give away free items!

Don't worry, this is not the boring, "canned" newsletter that most firms buy and add on their name. We write it ourselves to encourage people to pay more attention to their legal affairs.

If you later feel like you want to stop receiving our newsletter, there is a phone number in every issue that you can call to "unsubscribe."

To receive this newsletter, just photocopy this form, fill it out and e-mail or mail it to us. Email to: Newsletter@KevinMcManusLaw.com or mail to Kevin McManus, 1100 Main Street, Suite 2620, Kansas City, MO 64105.

Please send me your free legal newsletter:

Name:

____

Address:

____

City:_______________ State: ____ Zip: ____________

If you would like to receive our **email** newsletter, please include your email here:

E-mail:__________________________________

<u>We do not share mail/email lists with anyone!</u>

Made in the USA
Monee, IL
04 November 2026

67381841R10056